AN A L I E N S SEARCH-AND-FIND BOOK

FIND THE
XENOMORPH

FIND THE XENOMORPH

ISBN: 9781803362403
E-BOOK ISBN:9781803364322

Published by
Titan Books
A division of Titan Publishing Group Ltd
144 Southwark St
London
SE1 0UP

www.titanbooks.com

First edition: November 2023
10 9 8 7 6 5 4 3 2 1

Did you enjoy this book? We love to hear from our readers. Please e-mail us at: readerfeedback@titanemail.com or write to Reader Feedback at the above address.

To receive advance information, news, competitions, and exclusive offers online, please sign up for the Titan newsletter on our website: www.titanbooks.com

A CIP catalogue record for this title is available from the British Library.

Printed and bound in China.

AN **ALIENS** SEARCH-AND-FIND BOOK

FIND THE
XENOMORPH

ILLUSTRATED BY
KEVIN CROSSLEY

TITAN BOOKS

Welcome to the thrilling
and heart-pounding world
of *Find the Xenomorph*!
Are you ready to embark
on a pulse-pounding
search-and-find adventure
unlike any other? You are
about to be transported
straight into the gripping
and eerie world of the
abandoned colony of
Hadley's Hope, but with
a twist!

Get ready to join our
heroes on their daring
mission to find out exactly
what happened to the
people at the colony. But
beware, it won't be easy!
As you flip through the
pages, you'll be plunged
into atmospheric scenes
brought to life through

amazing illustrations that will keep you on the edge of your seat. From the dark and creepy corridors of the atmospheric processing plant to the treacherous and blood-soaked hallways of the *Sulaco*, every turn of the page will unveil a new challenge. Can you spot the Xenomorphs, colonists, weapons, and more lurking among the chaos?

There are 14 action-packed scenes to explore, so gear up, grab your pulse rifle, and get ready to embark on a hunt like no other in this gripping and visually stunning adventure. Good luck, but watch out—this time it's war!

BURSTING WITH FEAR

The first victims of Facehuggers returned to work, and seemed to recover after their ordeal. But when the Alien embryos burst from their chests, their colleagues can only stand around in a state of shock as the vicious infant creatures scurry away to hide.

CAN YOU FIND

x10

DON'T MAKE A SOUND...

The Xenomorph outbreak has decimated the population of Hadley's Hope. Most of the colonists have been taken by the creatures, but these otherworldly horrors are ever alert, always on the lookout for more victims...

CAN YOU FIND

x13

HIDE AND SEEK

The Xenomorph outbreak has completely overrun the atmospheric processing facility. Having killed or abducted most of the human colonists, the Alien creatures are unaware that a number of children have managed to avoid capture by doing what children do best: hiding!

CAN YOU FIND

x11

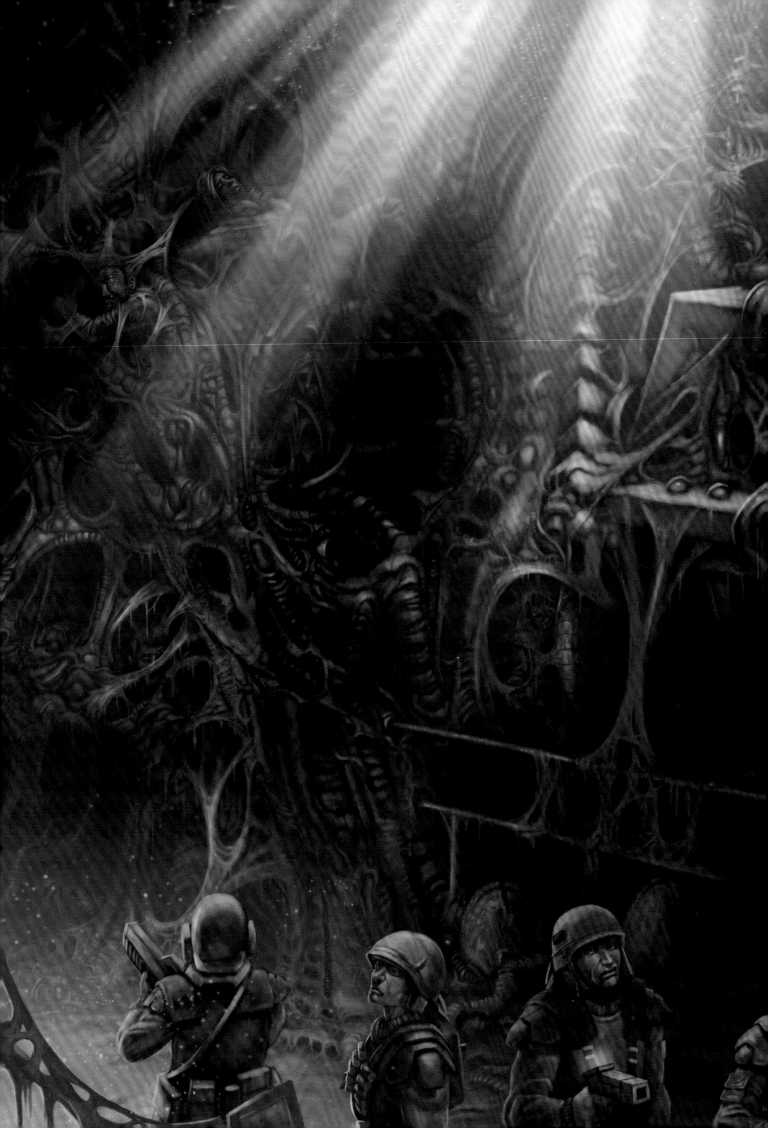

'WHAT HAPPENED HERE?'

In a gloomy part of the atmospheric processing facility, marines move cautiously through the industrial complex (now transformed into an unnatural, unearthly place) looking for the 'surviving' colonists.

CAN YOU FIND

x12

ENTOMBED BUT ALIVE

Having discovered
the location of most
of the colonists, it
seems to the marines
that most have met a
grisly end. However,
there are some who
still live...

CAN YOU FIND

x7

'THEY'RE COMING OUT OF THE WALLS!'

The marines walk warily through the facility, pulse rifles at the ready. The strange resin covers the walls, homoginizing machinery, piping, and conduits into an undulating Alien landscape. A perfect environment for the Alien creatures to hide themselves in.

CAN YOU FIND

x16

THIS TIME IT'S WAR!

The attack is on! The walls come alive as the marines suddenly find themselves in open battle with the vicious Alien creatures!

CAN YOU FIND

x20

CAN YOU FIND

x10

CAN YOU FIND

x15

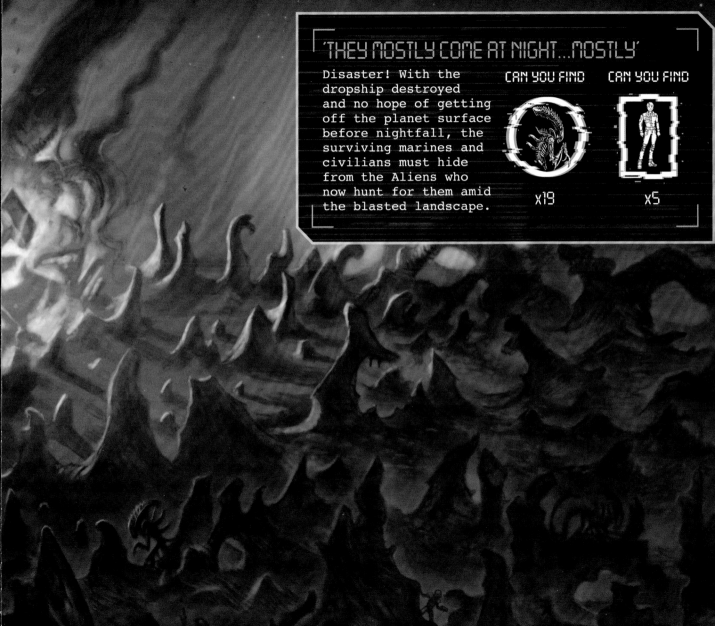

'THEY MOSTLY COME AT NIGHT...MOSTLY'

Disaster! With the dropship destroyed and no hope of getting off the planet surface before nightfall, the surviving marines and civilians must hide from the Aliens who now hunt for them amid the blasted landscape.

CAN YOU FIND

x19

CAN YOU FIND

x5

ARMS RACE

A handful of surviving marines have lost their weapons, but have found several of their fellow soldiers encased by the Xenomorphs in their strange resin. Luckily, some of the hapless victims were entombed with their pulse rifles. If only our heroes could find them, they might have a fighting chance to escape!

CAN YOU FIND

x11

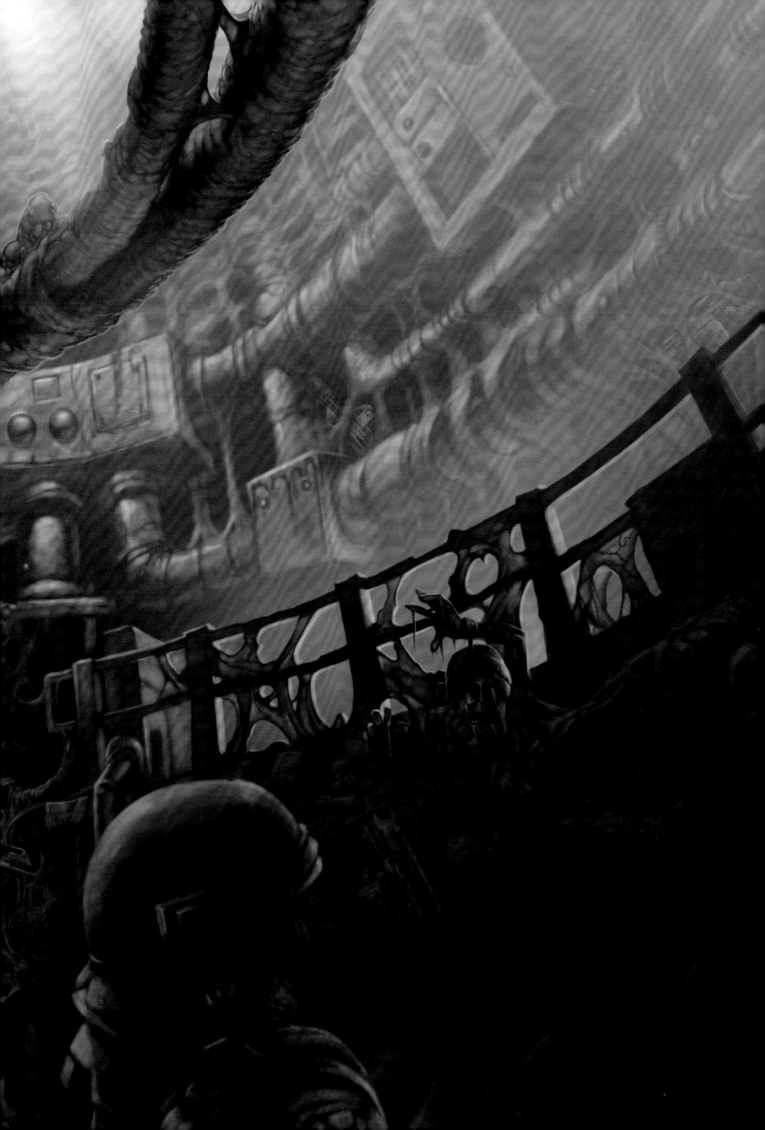

SHOOTING GALLERY

During an Alien assault, UA 571-C automated sentry guns killed most of the creatures. But a few remain, hiding among the corpses of their slaughtered kin...

CAN YOU FIND

X7

'WE'RE NOT ALONE...'

Two survivors have
found themselves
unexpectedly locked
inside the medical
bay with a handful of
Facehuggers that have
escaped their holding
tanks and are now hiding!

CAN YOU FIND

x9

'I MAY BE SYNTHETIC, BUT I'M NOT STUPID'

The android is making a dangerous journey to the communications tower to call in another dropship, but can he make it without being spotted by the Xenomorphs?

CAN YOU FIND
x8

CAN YOU FIND
x13

A DARING RESCUE!

The consultant has armed herself and has gone alone to find and rescue the sole child survivor of Hadley's Hope, who has been captured by the Aliens. She must be in here somewhere...

CAN YOU FIND x4

CAN YOU FIND x8

CAN YOU FIND x1

THE FINAL BATTLE!

It's a dramatic face-off in the *Sulaco*'s hangar as the final battle with the dreaded Alien Queen is about to begin!

CAN YOU FIND

CAN YOU FIND

x9

x9

SOLUTIONS

DON'T MAKE A SOUND...

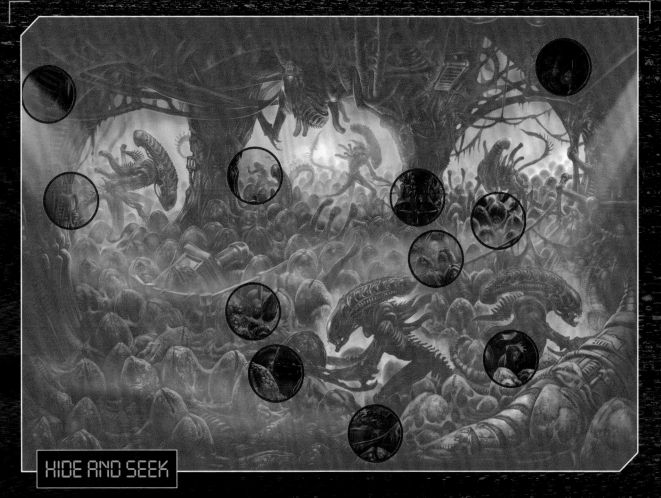

HIDE AND SEEK

'WHAT HAPPENED HERE?'

SOLUTIONS

ENTOMBED BUT ALIVE

'THEY'RE COMING OUT OF THE WALLS!'

'THEY MOSTLY COME AT NIGHT...MOSTLY'

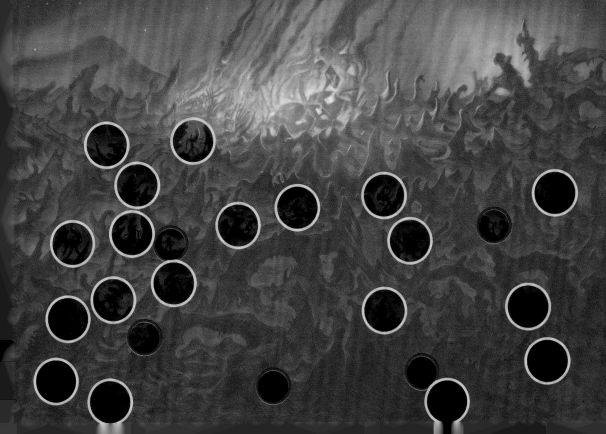

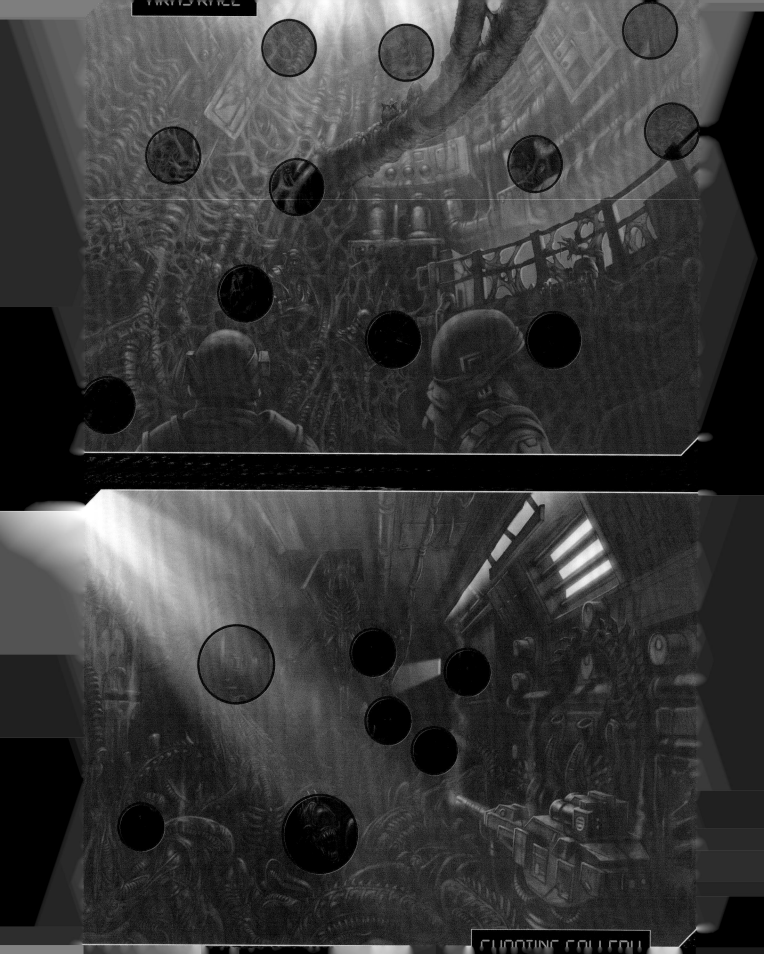

'WE'RE NOT ALONE...'

'I MAY BE SYNTHETIC, BUT I'M NOT STUPID'

SOLUTIONS

A DARING RESCUE!

THE FINAL BATTLE!